THE NATURE LIBRARY

CATS

YVONNE REES

CRESCENT BOOKS
NEW YORK

CLB 2582
© 1991 Colour Library Books Ltd., Godalming, Surrey, England.
All rights reserved.

This 1991 edition published by Crescent Books,
distributed by Outlet Book Company, Inc,
a Random House Company, 225 Park Avenue South,
New York, New York 10003.

Printed and bound in Hong Kong

ISBN 0-517-05153-2

8 7 6 5 4 3 2 1

Library of Congress Cataloging-in-Publication Data
Cats
    p. cm – (Nature Library)
    Includes index.
    Summary: Surveys the world of cats from ancient Egypt to the present,
including practical advice on caring for and breeding cats.
    ISBN 0-517-05153-2 : $6.99
    1. Cats – Juvenile literature.   (1. Cats.)   I. Series.
SF445.7.C39 1991   90-41178
636.8 – dc20   CIP
                                                           AC

Credits
Edited and designed: Ideas into Print, Vera Rogers and Stuart Watkinson
Layouts: Stonecastle Graphics Ltd. **Editorial assistance:** Joanne King
Picture Editors: Annette Lerner, John Kaprielian
Photographs: Photo Researchers Inc. New York, and Marc Henrie
Commissioning Editor: Andrew Preston
Production: Ruth Arthur, Sally Connolly, David Proffit, Andrew Whitelaw
Director of Production: Gerald Hughes
Director of Publishing: David Gibbon
Typesetting: SX Composing Ltd.
Color separations: Scantrans Pte. Ltd., Singapore

The Author
Yvonne Rees is a writer and lecturer on a wide range of subjects, including
wildlife and animals. She shares her home in the country with a variety of
domestic animals (and many wild ones), including two cats and two dogs.
Looking after pets for friends and neighbors has involved Yvonne in
keeping an eye on anything from quails and peacocks to cats, dogs, goats,
hens and sheep. In her spare time she likes to paint, and has often turned
her hand to preparing pet portraits for proud owners.

CONTENTS

Above: Some expressions say it all. This house cat has the look of a pet with ambitions to rule the world, but perhaps not today while everything at home is just fine and dandy. Perhaps tomorrow.

Left: An elegant Havana Brown in a typically inquiring pose. These lithe and active cats are gentle by nature and make attractive and loving pets. This is just one of many shorthaired breeds with a Siamese-type of body.

ANCESTORS OF THE DOMESTIC CAT

One of the pleasures of owning a cat is to watch it stalking through rough grass outside, or hunting an invisible mouse in the house, and to imagine its wild relatives: the prehistoric sabre-toothed tiger or today's leopard. The resemblance is still so strong, and the basic instincts of survival remain so evident, that it is almost like owning a smaller version of these wild and beautiful creatures.

We know that one of the cat's earliest ancestors was the, now extinct, sabre-toothed tiger that lived about 35 million years ago. A fierce and strongly built animal, the sabre-tooth used its daggerlike fangs to stab and kill its prey. Fossil remains have proved that, from about 12 million years ago, there were also smaller cats, very like our present-day domestic pets.

By the time of the Ice Age, three million years ago, the three groups of cat we are familiar with today were well established: big cats, such as lions and tigers (*Panthera*); smaller cats like our pets (*Felis*); and cheetahs, whose claws do not retract (*Acinonyx*). It is interesting to know that all of today's household cats, from whatever part of the world, probably spring from one ancestral species: the African wild cat (*Felis libyca*). Later, cross-breeding with the European wild cat (*Felis sylvestris*) produced the popular tabby markings and stockier body, to be seen in today's British Shorthair and Persian breeds. There is also an elegant wild jungle cat (*Felis chaus*) believed to be the type of cat domesticated by the Egyptians.

All these wild, or feral, cats survive today, little changed from their ancestors and living not only in the wilder parts of the world, but also close to towns and cities. In fact, domestic cats often run away and become wild or breed with feral cats.

Below: Sabre-toothed tigers *(Smilodon californicus)* died out towards the end of the Ice Age to be replaced by the sleeker, more intelligent ancestors of today's domestic cat.

Right: Reconstructed remains of the sabre-toothed tiger reveal a weighty body and huge jaws, designed to stab rather than bite prey.

Above: The tiger is one of the big cats in the *Panthera* genus. It is the only truly striped wild cat, and the largest surviving member of the family. Some are white with light brown stripes.

Left: The black striped tabby European wild cat *(Felis silvestris)* found across Europe and western Asia, is possibly an ancestor of the domestic cat.

Above: Among the small wild cats (those that cannot roar), the cheetah *(Acinonyx jubatus)* is put in a class of its own because it cannot retract its claws.

Right: The lynx *(Felis lynx)* is a light brown spotted wild cat with tufted ears and a short tail. It lives in northern forests across the world.

Above: The early carnivores (Carnivora) could be divided into doglike animals, such as wolves and foxes, and catlike creatures, including civets, mongooses and, as shown here, genets.

Right: Native to tropical forest areas, the jaguar *(Panthera onca)* is the largest American wild cat. It has a spotted coat, perfect for forest camouflage, although some are darker and look almost totally black.

DOMESTIC CATS IN ANCIENT TIMES

The Egyptians were probably the first to tame cats and keep them as domestic animals, in around 3000 BC. The cats were originally intended to work for their living, keeping vermin such as rats and mice under control. (This job was once carried out, in Europe at least, by weasels.) However, it was not long before their graceful and affectionate nature won them a new role in the home, as loved and valued pets. In Egypt, cats were worshipped as gods, and archaeologists have found many Ancient Egyptian cat statues and mummified cats. They embalmed their cats and wrapped them in fine linen before burying them in a plain or cat-shaped coffin; excavations have uncovered whole cat cemeteries along the Nile.

The Egyptians guarded their cats carefully and forbade their export, but they soon spread to the Middle East, India and China in the baggage of travellers and traders. In China, the baskets and cages of cats that began to appear in the markets were often intended for the dinner table. The Japanese, however, valued cats for their skill at hunting mice. In homes and at the Royal Palace, where they were fed the best tidbits and led on silken leads, cats became so prized that there were not enough left to hunt mice in city granaries and food stores. When these became over-run with vermin, Japan started a deliberate breeding programme and made it law that all cats be set free.

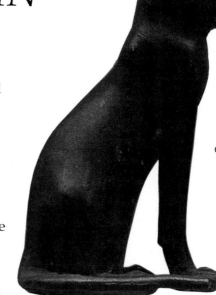

Left: From the large number of sacred statues that have been found, we know that cats were worshipped as gods in Ancient Egypt. This figure of Bast, the cat goddess, is from the ancient city of Bubastis, where the Great Cat Temple was situated.

Right: Tomb paintings are proof that cats were kept as domestic pets and hunting companions in Ancient Egypt. In this picture, found at Thebes and dated about 1400 BC, a large tabby is depicted accompanying a hunt for wild birds.

Surviving mosaic pictures and writings show that the Romans were the first keen European cat lovers. Their armies first brought back cats from abroad, and subsequently cats would accompany the army wherever it travelled. In this way, pet cats became even more widespread and began to interbreed with local feral cats. Later, European explorers and traders began to bring domestic cats back from all parts of the world, paying their passage by keeping down vermin aboard ship en route. The Crusaders were largely responsible for bringing back long-coated, exotically coloured cats when they returned from the Holy Wars during the 11th to the 13th centuries.

Left: Fierce lion-type statues and elaborately carved and painted figures outside ancient oriental palaces imply a sacred status. This gold figure stands guard at the Chinese Summer Palace in Peking.

Left: Countless cats were embalmed and mummified by the Ancient Egyptians. They were laid in elaborately carved wooden coffins or wrapped in plaited straw, to be stored at the Great Temple of Bast at Bubastis.

Right: This bronze figure of Bast, or Pasht, was found at Bubastis and has a cat's head on a female body. A group of kittens sit at her feet. The name Pasht is said to be the origin of our word 'puss'.

Above: Cats seem to have played a favoured or ritual role in ancient cults, as this strikingly carved and painted Mexican Indian cat mask shows.

Below: The front legs of the hairless Sphynx are longer than the hind legs. It is this cat's curious posture that probably accounts for the common name.

Above: The elegant Abyssinian, with its long slender body, long tail and large pointed ears, is believed to have descended directly from the Sacred Cat of Ancient Egypt.

ANATOMY OF THE CAT

The cat's wonderfully refined anatomy gives it agility and those special skills designed to ensure its survival in the wild. Its very body shape – lithe and graceful with a small head but extremely powerful hind quarters and back – gives the cat speed, agility and an excellent sense of balance. These qualities allow cats to climb up to, and move along, narrow and high places out of danger – cats can jump up to five times their own height – and make them superb hunters. A cat can flatten itself to the ground to observe prey, move quickly and silently, then pounce with deadly accuracy. It is one of the few creatures to have retractable claws. When they are withdrawn, a cat can walk silently and easily on its pads, with no risk of damage; with the claws out, it is a fighter to be reckoned with.

Keenly developed senses of smell, hearing and sight also help to make the cat a quick and efficient hunter. Its ears are especially sensitive to high-frequency sounds, so that it can pick up the squeaking of small mammals, such as rodents, and correctly identify the exact source of the sounds. Sight is particularly good at night, which is when cats are normally most active. They cannot see perfectly in the dark, but given a glimmer, their vision is good enough to distinguish shapes and movements much more clearly than we can. If a cat becomes deaf, its sight and sense of smell are sharpened to compensate. Every part of the body is specifically refined to its purpose: the teeth are sensitive and extremely precise, locating exactly the right point before they bite; and the tongue is long and muscular, capable of scooping up liquids as efficiently as a spoon, yet rough enough to give the cat's coat a good grooming.

Above: Excellent sight, smell and hearing are essential to the cat's role as predatory hunter. The forwardly pricked ears, large eyes and alert expression indicate a constant awareness of its surroundings.

Above: Kittens grow quickly and explore their essential senses and instincts from a very early age. Sight and muscular coordination develop from about the third week.

Right: Superb muscle control and coordination give the cat grace and speed. Even the skeleton is specially adapted to allow movement and good balance: a reduced size collar bone and narrow chest means that it can negotiate small spaces and narrow ledges. A very flexible backbone also allows a cat to stretch its body into a wide variety of postures or curl up into a complete circle. Big thigh muscles give the animal its leaping power.

Right: A cat's sense of taste and smell are closely linked, since the nasal passage opens into the mouth. A cat will use its nose constantly as a backup to its sense of sight to identify any unfamiliar object or person. It will sniff food thoroughly, for example, before deciding whether it is safe to eat.

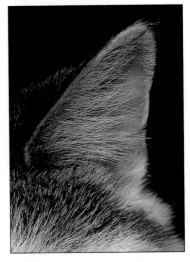

Right: Cats are very agile. Their strong hind legs enable them to jump up to five times their own height. The flexible tail, with as many as 28 small vertebrae, is essential for balance. The front paws are capable of a wide range of tasks, from opening doors to pouncing on prey.

Above: The jaw is muscular and flexible. The teeth are designed to kill, to tear flesh, rip, scrape and cut meat into pieces. The tongue can be made into a spoon shape for lapping liquids.

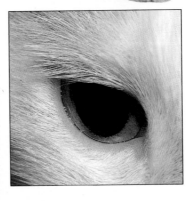

Above: Good vision is perhaps the cat's best sense. Eye colour varies from yellow and orange to green, blue and mauve.

Left: A mobile backbone means a cat can rotate the front half of the spine through an angle of 180° in relation to its back half.

Above: A cat can hear with extraordinary accuracy, which is important for locating small prey and to sense any likely danger.

CAT-NAPPING AND OTHER HABITS

'Curiosity killed the cat', according to the proverb, and cats certainly live up to their reputation for being nosy. They will pry into nearly everything that catches their attention, with no apparent thought for their own safety – from loud machinery to a basket of knitting wools. Even the fattest, laziest cat will prick up its ears and twitch its whiskers with interest at a new sound, sight or scent. They love to explore and play. Grown cats sometimes display quite kittenish acrobatics – much to the delight of their owners – which can lead them into mischief.

Cats like to have their own way, and will not be persuaded to sit on a lap or stay indoors if they prefer to do otherwise. Yet cats are surprisingly adaptable, settling down with almost any other animal and in most types of environment, so long as they feel they are in charge. They are generally affectionate creatures and love being spoiled and petted, when they will roll and purr appreciatively. They can also be nasty and bad tempered, especially towards an intruder, and have been known to actually pounce on and scratch a stranger, particularly if a queen is nursing kittens.

In contrast to all this energetic activity, cats prefer to sleep much of the day – usually in short bursts, hence the expression cat-napping – and usually in the warmest spot they can find. This may not always seem the most comfortable. A cat perched on top of a post or wall in the garden may look precarious, but in full sunshine, with one eye open for danger, its elevated position makes a good vantage point. For cats are always alert to the slightest danger, even when asleep. In summer, they will settle down in the coolness of long grass or under a shady bush, as camouflaged as their wild cousins the lions and tigers. In winter, they will curl up in their basket, or lie so close to the stove or fire that you will smell singed fur before they move. Cats hate to be wet, and will stay indoors, or shelter in a shed or outhouse on rainy days.

Left: Thoroughly contented cats will happily sleep alongside their owners, where they enjoy the feeling of warmth and security.

Right: Cats, particularly kittens, always seem to enjoy sleeping together, especially if they are part of the same litter. They will look like a single large ball of fur, all curled up together.

Left: Most domestic cats spend the greater part of their day either resting or sleeping. This is because they are naturally most active during the night, as is clear from their familiar calls.

Below: Young adult cats will continue to sleep together, as this gives them both the warmth and sense of comfort and companionship they seek. They only need to be supplied with one bed or sleeping place in which they can feel secure.

Below: Every time a cat awakes, it automatically stretches to flex every muscle and sinew to its fullest extent and restore circulation.

Above: Sometimes, cats will sit so close to the fire that their fur singes before they will move away.

Right: A cat rudely awakened or frightened while sleeping will face the offender by snarling and spitting with teeth bared. These are instinctive warning signals.

INSTINCTIVE BEHAVIOUR

Cats' instincts are highly developed from the earliest age. When only several weeks old, they will begin to go through the primeval motions of hunting, establishing a territory, fighting and claw sharpening. They are also remarkably sensitive, quickly picking up on any change of mood in their owners, and becoming distressed or attempting to comfort them if they sense they are depressed or unhappy. Their hunting instinct is quite remarkable, combining a tireless patience for keeping watch or stalking, with acute senses of sight, smell and hearing that enable them to locate and pounce on prey with amazing accuracy. They are also excellent climbers, with a complete lack of fear for heights, and will use their claws and superb sense of balance to scale walls, fences, posts and trees – sometimes to a point from which they think they cannot get down again. However, rescue is not normally necessary; leave a wailing cat up a tree for a few hours and it usually finds a way back to safety. Luckily a cat's dangerous love of heights is balanced by its incredible ability to land on its feet after a jump or fall. It does this by what is called the 'self-reflecting reflex' – the body instinctively turns in a spiral of up to 180° to land with the feet downwards.

Cats are also strongly territorial – they like to mark out the boundaries of what they consider to be their patch, and will protect that area fiercely should anything threaten it. This causes problems in towns

Below: A cat sharpens its claws not only to remove any snags or loose scales, but also to leave a mark for other cats to see. If your cat does not have access to trees and posts outdoors, it will resort to your furniture.

and cities, where the patch might be very small indeed. Male cats have an annoying habit of marking their territory by spraying with strong-smelling urine – you will see visiting cats picking up on such scents by curling their lip and smelling. Unexpectedly confronted by an intruder or another cat, a cat will stand its ground, even when faced by a much bigger animal. Arching the back and fluffing out the fur is intended to make the cat look bigger as it braces its body ready to scratch and claw. An angry or frightened cat will also open its mouth wide to bare the fangs, hissing or spitting to increase the impact of the intimidating display.

Left: A cat that has been startled or set upon unawares will make itself look much bigger by fluffing up its fur.

Above: As part of the mating ritual, a female cat will tread with her front paws and raise her tail while mewing repeatedly.

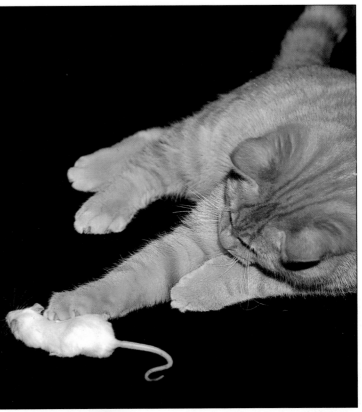

Above: A cat can seem rather cruel in the way it enjoys playing with a mouse or shrew, patting it with its paws for some while and keeping the small animal within reach before finally killing it, but this is instinctive behaviour.

Below: There is hardly any obstacle that a cat cannot negotiate safely, for it can rely on its superbly designed body and instinctive sense of balance to guide it across dangerously high or narrow places.

Above: Cats have an amazing ability to save themselves from falling on their backs. As they fall, they jack knife the body and use the tail to land on all four paws without overbalancing.

Right: A cat will perch on the most uncomfortable looking fencepost, narrow wall or rooftop because they offer such excellent vantage points.

A CAT FOR YOU

You would love a cat – or maybe two, but with such a wide variety of shapes, colours and characters, how do you choose the ideal companion for you and your home? It may be that the luxury of choice is taken away from you. You could be adopted by a stray, be given a cat as a gift or agree to care for an existing adult should the owner have to move away. Often, a friend or neighbour will have a litter of kittens they are trying to place, or you will see an advertisement begging good homes.

Whatever their breed and parentage, all kittens are appealing and difficult to resist. So if you want a cat for a specific purpose, or conditions at home demand a certain type of cat, do not be seduced into taking on an unsuitable pet. If you want a pure pedigree or you are hoping to breed from your cat, then you must be prepared to buy from an accredited dealer and to pay a good price. In this case, you will no doubt have some idea of the breed you prefer, and will have researched its habits, needs and any special treatment it might require. If you are simply seeking a pet, buying a cat from a pet shop may be relatively cheaper, yet still give you plenty of choice. Acquiring a young kitten or abandoned adult from your local cat protection society, in return for a donation, is another sensible way to find a friend and help the local feline population. You should check that the cat is lively, with no visible signs of disease or distress; ask the advice of a veterinarian if you have any doubts.

Finding a cat that appeals to you is the easy part, but is it a type that is going to be happy with you? If it must be shut up indoors all day, try to avoid breeds like the Maine Coon that need plenty of exercise. Many people make the mistake of taking on a beautiful longhaired variety without realizing the amount of extra work this entails – daily grooming can be essential to keep them in good condition, for example. A longhaired cat will also shed a lot of fur around the house. A young kitten may not be the best choice if you do not have the time to give it plenty of attention during the first months of its life, or if you have a new baby, or if you value your furniture and furnishings. In this instance, you might be better advised to take on a quiet, unwanted adult cat, already house-trained and placid by nature. This would be ideal for the elderly.

Below: Persians, with their long silky fur and fine colouring, are beautiful pets, but only suitable for people prepared to tackle the daily grooming or who want to show their cat.

Above: A placid, good-natured cat is best for an elderly owner looking for a loving but intelligent companion. When buying a new pet, consider choosing a mature, trained cat.

Left: Giving children a cat of their own to look after teaches them a sense of responsibility and encourages them to build up a mutual relationship of love and trust with their companion.

Right: Most cats are very adaptable and happy in a country house or city apartment. Owners in busy areas may be reluctant to let their pets out if the traffic is heavy.

Left: Owners of pedigree cats are justifiably proud of their desirable pets. This purebred Abyssinian kitten is clearly going to be spoiled by its keeper.

Above: When buying a kitten, try to see the whole litter with their mother to ensure they are healthy and well cared for. Choice of colour and character will be a purely personal one.

Right: Loving but independent, and thus easier to look after than a pet dog, a cat in the home will delight all members of the family, without taking up too much of their time.

COPING WITH A NEW KITTEN

A new baby in the house is sure to cause disruptions and a young animal is no exception. The best way to cope is to make sure you have everything you need to hand right from the start. And then to establish a regular routine. Proper care and reassurance in these early days will affect the behaviour and habits of your cat for the rest of its life. Try to give your kitten as much attention as possible when it is first introduced to your home, confining it to one room until it has found its bearings and not startling it with loud noises or too many people at one time. You should teach every member of the family, even young toddlers, how to pick up and hold it correctly, with its weight firmly and comfortably supported.

Your kitten will spend a lot of time sleeping and you should provide it with some form of bed, such as its own wicker or glassfibre basket, or simply a cardboard box. Line the bed with newspaper and an old towel or blanket for warmth. Also vital from day one while your cat is housebound is a litter tray – made of easy-to-clean metal, glassfibre or plastic and containing sand, soil or commercially prepared litter; make sure you change this regularly. Later, you can train your cat to use a door flap if you have outdoor facilities. Provide food and water bowls on a mat or newspaper for easy cleaning should spills occur; you will need to feed your cat at regular intervals at first, maybe three or four times a day according to the breeder's or previous owner's recommendations.

To save unnecessary suffering, have your kitten inoculated by the local veterinarian, as recommended, against the most dangerous infectious cat diseases from the age of about two months. And unless you are intending to breed from your cat, neutering at five to six months is a good idea to prevent unwanted pregnancies and encourage a more docile, sociable nature. Always transport your cat in a properly designed cardboard, metal, plastic or wicker carrier.

Left: For the first few weeks of its life, your kitten will be totally dependent on its mother and she will attend to all its physical and instinctive needs.

Right: Given plenty of love and attention, a young kitten will quickly form a bond of trust and friendship with its owner.

Below: Learn how to lift and hold your cat correctly to avoid distressing or damaging it; use one hand to support the chest and the other to take the weight of its hind legs.

Left: A young kitten is delightful and appealing, but you must be prepared to provide the care and attention it needs during the early months of its young life.

Above: The mother should teach her kitten how to use the litter tray, but it will soon get the idea if you put it in and show it how to scratch the litter material.

Above: Kittens need a warm, draught-free place to sleep, where they will snuggle down in straw or on a blanket.

Above: Beds suitable for one or more kittens may be made of wood, plastic, basketwork or bean-filled fabric.

FROM KITTEN TO CAT

A young kitten is a delight to watch around the house or garden – exploring, playing and trying out new experiences and skills from a surprisingly early age. Make the most of these early months – cats grow and develop so quickly. If you have a camera, take plenty of photographs before they grow up – you will find kittens a wonderful natural subject, forever tumbling, investigating new objects or peeping appealingly out of baskets, bins and bags. If you have more than one kitten, this only increases the fun – and your pleasure as onlooker – as they indulge in madcap games, mock fights and other brother and sister activities.

Play begins at around five weeks old, before the kitten has left its mother. This is the time you will also observe it attempting to groom itself. It has all its milk teeth by eight weeks, by which time most kittens will have started to develop their hunting instincts, stalking a screwed up ball of paper across the kitchen floor or pouncing on your shoelace, a toy or a fellow kitten. You can encourage these games by dangling pieces of string, or twitching toy mice out of reach, to help develop the familiar hunting actions of swatting (later to be tried out on moths and small birds), scooping with the paws – for catching fish, and pouncing on rodents. Even a young kitten can be extremely quick and surprisingly accurate, so try not to use your hands and feet for mock hunting games, if you wish to avoid sharp scratches. Do not worry if you have a couple of kittens that seem to be fighting a little too fiercely – growling, pouncing, rolling and biting each other's necks; this is only normal rough and tumble. Such chasing, wrestling and boxing will help develop their natural skills, and give them valuable exercise through play.

Above: Kittens love to play, and as well as being amusing for their owners to watch, it is good stimulation and exercise for them. You can provide small toys for kittens to play with.

Right: Even young kittens are adventurous and will boldy climb to the top of the nearest tree when allowed outdoors for the first time, exploring new muscles and abilities.

Above: A solitary cat will find plenty to amuse it, especially in the garden, where it will learn to develop many new physical and instinctive skills, such as climbing, jumping and hunting.

Above left: A mother cat will encircle her newly born kittens to encourage them to suckle.

Above: At just four weeks old, kittens will start wrestling, clasping with their front paws and kicking with their hind legs.

Below: Mock fights between young cats seem aggressive but are never serious. Each takes it in turn to be the aggressor, swatting, chasing and neck biting.

A CAT IN THE HOUSE

Most cats are well-loved and practical house pets. They are small, adaptable to almost any house or apartment and make a loving companion to owners of all ages – an animal that visibly enjoys the home comforts of a soft lap or a warm fire. You can easily train them to use a door flap, and to come and go as they please when access to a garden or backyard is available. This releases you from the chore of ensuring that your pet has adequate fresh air and exercise. If this is not possible, which can be the situation in high-rise blocks or in built-up town and city areas, your cat may be completely housebound, in which case you must be sure to provide toilet facilities in the form of a litter tray or enclosed box, which must be emptied regularly. Some breeds of cat are better suited to an indoor life than others: Somali and Abyssinian cats, for example, really need access to the outdoors.

Your cat will need somewhere to sleep – an old cardboard box, a wicker or plastic basket, a piece of blanket or a dresser kennel would all be acceptable – providing that you do not keep changing its position, and that it is warm and cosy, away from any draughts. Of course, cats are remarkably independent, and yours may prefer to sleep on the foot of your bed or curled round the stove – it is up to you whether you are happy with this arrangement, or whether you want to be firm and discourage the practice. Good door catches may be necessary to keep cats out of rooms where they are not supposed to be – they can be surprisingly adept at getting heavy doors open with their paws.

You may also need to consider other drawbacks of having a cat in the house – cat hairs, for example, particularly from longhair breeds. Ornaments, pet fish and caged birds may be at risk, as may houseplants, especially if the cat is completely housebound and deprived of grass to nibble. Some plants, such as ivies and philodendrons, are poisonous to cats. Cats are terribly curious, with a complete disregard for their own safety, and so other danger areas include open fires, plastic bags and poisonous substances. Cats will need to be trained not to bite electric cables or to jump up on stoves or cooking hobs.

Left: A cat flap means your cat has free access to fresh air and the outdoors, making it very little trouble to look after in the home.

Above: A cat in the house can be as comforting as an open fire and a rewarding and extremely loving companion for the housebound.

Left: A cat left alone in the house will soon get into mischief if you do not tidy away 'toys', such as balls of string.

Right: A house cat will use the simplest items, such as a screwed up ball of paper, for mock hunting games.

Above: Some owners do not mind sharing their bed with their pet; others discourage it on hygienic grounds. It could be dangerous for young children.

Below: Ever curious, a cat will want to be part of your everyday life, which is not always welcome if you work from home!

Above: Deprived of the chance to nibble greenery outdoors, a housebound cat may munch houseplants. Ideally, provide pots of homegrown grass.

THE OUTDOOR LIFE

Below: In the garden there are plenty of diversions to keep a cat alert and lively.

Even the smallest garden will offer a cat hours of fun and valuable exercise. It becomes its territory, to be marked out and defended, especially in towns, where space is limited and the local cat population high. A shrubbery or long grass is a miniature jungle. There are birds and butterflies to stalk, mice, shrews and other small rodents to catch, and countless sunny spots to enjoy dozing in – from a fence or brick wall to the highest of rooftops. For the housebound city cat, outdoors might be restricted to a balcony or 'cat perch' attached to the windowsill which, in high-rise properties, must be protected with wire to prevent falls. Some owners like to give housebound cats outdoor exercise on a lead, but this is only really practical with docile, shorthaired breeds, such as Siamese and Burmese, that can be 'walked' like a dog. Cats are never as easy to train as a dog, and should be introduced to the lead as a young kitten. Even then, you will never be able to force a cat to take to a collar and lead if it does not want to.

If the surrounding area is full of hazards, such as busy traffic, it is possible to contain cats in an outdoor run or pen – a large wooden or steel framework fitted with strong wire mesh, including the roof area. Ensure that the pen is big enough to allow the cat (or cats) plenty of freedom, with an arrangement of shelves for sunning themselves and jumping exercises, a tree or post for climbing and scratching, and some form of shelter for wet days. If the pen is providing outdoor facilities for a house cat, butt it onto the house wall and provide access directly via a cat flap. A small pen is sufficient if your cat will only be taking a couple of hours exercise there. Where it provides more permanent accommodation – for an un-neutered tom, perhaps, that can smell rather strong indoors – it will need to be larger and include some form of heating for periods of cold weather.

Below: Body rubbing and sniffing are all part of an identification and security routine for kittens out with their mother for the first time.

Above: Wild cats naturally live in groups, and even kittens from different litters will grow up to play and live happily together, providing they are introduced to each other at an early age.

Below: Trees offer the chance to develop essential climbing and balancing skills. Cats may be lured to great heights in the hope of catching a bird.

Above: Country cats and kittens are often kept outdoors all the time to keep rodents, such as rats and mice, under control.

Left: With their natural feline inquisitiveness, cats can find hours of fun in the garden.

CARING FOR YOUR CAT

Strongly independent and well equipped to look after themselves, cats require far less care and attention than many other pets. These highly intelligent animals can be trained to carry out routine procedures for themselves: to come and go as they please; to be toilet trained; and to take adequate exercise. However, unless your cat is partly wild or has always lived in a very remote country area and been left to fend for itself, like some communities of farm cats, there are tasks which you must not neglect. Indeed, to maintain a healthy, happy cat, you must undertake certain care routines seriously and carry them out on a strictly regular basis.

Feeding should provide a good balanced diet of protein in the form of meat or fish, plus vegetables and fats, as well as carbohydrates in the form of bread and cereals. A mineral supplement should not be necessary, unless the animal is sick, pregnant or nursing young. Although pre-packed cat foods – canned, pelleted or dried – claim to provide a balanced diet, fresh food is recommended twice a week for good health. Plenty of water is essential, and a clean supply should be permanently available. Milk is a useful source of minerals and protein, but some cats are allergic to it. A sensible diet, plenty of exercise and annual visits to your veterinarian for routine inoculations should keep a cat fit and healthy.

Whether you are moving house or taking a short trip across town, always transport your cat in a proper carrier – usually made of plastic, fibreglass, cardboard or wickerwork. It is a good idea to attach a name and address tag to your cat's collar, just in case it should escape, especially if you are travelling any distance. Cats have a wonderful homing instinct, believed to be based on the angle of the sun at certain times of the day, and will often trek hundreds of miles back to the former home after a move. For this reason, some owners, sadly, have to leave their pets behind when they move away from the district.

Below: The right food and a regular feeding routine are essential. Give your cat its own dish or bowl and do not change its position.

Right: Use a proper carrying case or basket, even for small kittens. To put a cat into a carrier, quieten it first by stroking and petting it, then grasp it by the scruff of the neck, supporting its weight with a hand under the rear before lifting it in.

Left: Your cat should enjoy plenty of love and attention from all members of the family. Take the time to stroke and pet it and it will reward you by developing a quiet and affectionate nature.

Right: Lift a grown cat with care to prevent hurting it. Support both the front and rear of the body from below to discourage the cat struggling.

Above: For the housebound cat, providing the fresh greenery it needs to maintain good health can be a problem, but you can grow lawn grass or cereal, such as oats or wheat, in trays or pots.

Right: In a small home, it may be more convenient to keep a litter of young kittens in a special pen.

Below: Sprays and powders control flea infestations. You will probably need to make this a regular routine. Spray carpets and the cat bed, too.

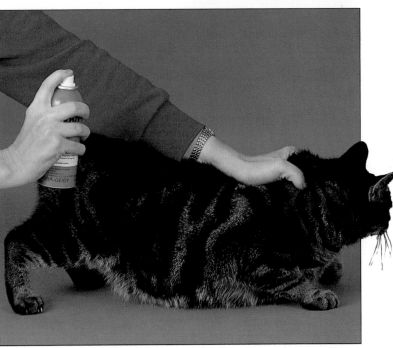

GROOMING YOUR CAT

Cats are remarkably good at cleaning themselves, and you will see them spending a large part of the day keeping the coat glossy and in good condition. Their rough, strong tongues are specially designed to remove dust and dirt, dead hair and skin, as well as toning up the muscles of the body and keeping the cat generally flexible. A young kitten that has been removed from its mother too early may not have developed these skills very well, and will need a little encouragement. Dabbing some butter on its paws and inaccessible parts may act as an encouragement, or a fellow cat may step in to teach the correct lessons.

Although a cat does a good job for itself, a little extra grooming is helpful to keep your cat in tip-top condition – essential if it is a longhaired breed. A regular inspection and cleaning routine is also a good idea to keep a check on possible ailments. Gently wipe the dirt away from the eye area, for example, using a wad moistened in warm water. You may need to trim the cat's claws if it is confined indoors much of the day, and you should clean the teeth every week to prevent build-up of tartar.

Shorthaired cats need to be groomed only twice a week. This is a good opportunity to look out for flea infestation, visible as black or brown specks. First, comb the cat from head to tail with a fine-toothed metal comb or soft natural bristle brush. Conditioner, rubbed into the coat after grooming, removes grease

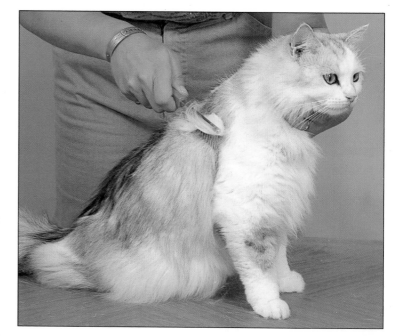

Above: Longhaired breeds are the most difficult to groom and it takes longer to get them back into good condition if neglected.

Right: Shorthaired cats should be groomed with a double-sided bristle or rubber brush, working from the head towards the tail.

and brings out the colour of the coat. For the really proud owner, a final polish with a chamois cloth produces a lovely shine.

Longhair cats need daily grooming, or their fur becomes matted and dull. Use a wide-toothed comb to tease out hair balls, and then a wire brush to remove all the dead hair – longhairs tend to moult profusely. Some talcum powder or fuller's earth brushed through the coat helps to separate the hairs. Run a fine-toothed comb through the hair in an upwards motion to give the fur a final fluff-up.

Below: Most cats thoroughly enjoy a gentle brushing. As long as you brush in the direction of the hair, they will normally purr contentedly and flex their claws.

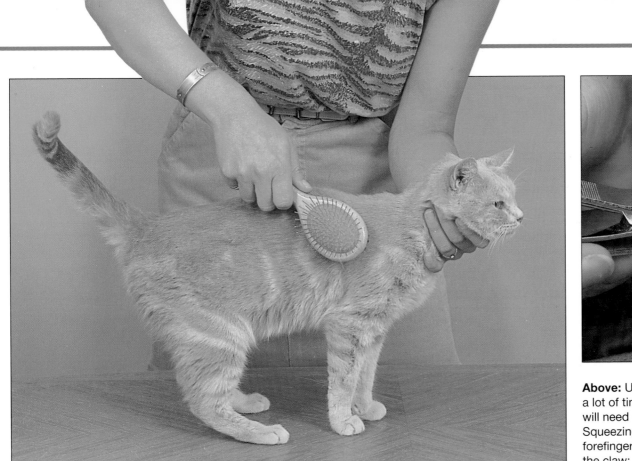

Above: Unless your cat spends a lot of time outdoors, the claws will need clipping regularly. Squeezing the toe between the forefinger and thumb will extend the claw: only remove the tip.

Right: It is best to get your cat used to being bathed at the earliest age. A rubber mat in the bottom of your basin or bowl will give a better grip. Use baby or pet shampoo and avoid the ears.

Below: To produce a final shine on a shorthaired cat's coat after grooming, giving it a gentle rub down with a cloth or chamois leather will get rid of any of the finer loose hairs.

TRAINING YOUR CAT

A cat's supreme intelligence is legendary, making it quick to learn and highly adaptable. With patient and consistent training, especially at the kitten stage, any cat will quickly learn routine tasks, such as using a litter tray or cat flap. However, cats are equally capable of working things out for themselves, and will constantly surprise their owners by climbing up and drinking from a dripping tap when thirsty, or squatting over the bath plughole when accidently shut in the house without litter facilities. A great many cats will rap at the door or window to be let in. Some even teach themselves to open the door of the refrigerator.

The household cat has many extra skills to learn in order to become an acceptable member of the family. Most are very good at using a litter tray from kittenhood – providing it is emptied regularly, as cats are fastidious. The house cat must also learn not to scratch the furniture – you should offer an alternative, such as a scratching post. Discourage un-neutered cats from spraying urine around the house as a form of territory marking. If castrating is not possible or desired, squirting the cat with water when caught in the act may be enough to get the message across. If you have the patience, you can train cats to perform tricks for your own amusement. A useful 'trick' is for a cat to come when it is called. You should teach the cat

its name when it is a kitten. Then reward it with petting or food when it responds to the name being called and the command 'come'. By using rewards you can train your cat to sit, beg, even jump through a hoop, providing you have the patience to keep repeating every step of the procedure until the cat has understood the instruction and learned it.

Above: Urine spraying or scent marking is one way a cat will establish territorial boundaries. The scent is unpleasantly 'catty' but is only really noticeable in an un-neutered tom cat. While it will not be noticed on your garden fences and bushes, if the cat starts doing it indoors it can be a nuisance. If you have a tom cat and are not intending to breed him, then castration is the best solution to the problem.

Left: Cats scratch to sharpen their front claws and also to leave a marker to be seen by other cats. To teach your pet not to destroy your furniture and woodwork, you will need to show it how to use its claws on a scratching post as a kitten. Later, if a cat has access to a garden, it should naturally use surrounding trees and posts. A strong smelling polish may also act as a deterrent indoors.

Right: Kittens quickly learn to use a litter tray and will continue to use it correctly providing you clean it regularly.

Below: Providing they are trained from an early age, cats can be taught to perform a wide range of amusing tricks. They will also learn useful techniques for themselves, such as drinking from a tap when thirsty.

Below: A cat flap allows your cat to come and go at will, and means it can be trained to go outdoors rather than use a litter tray. Pushing the cat through both ways a few times is usually enough for it to grasp the idea. Some doors operate magnetically from the collar.

Right: Cats have an inbuilt homing instinct and they rarely wander off and get lost. They may disappear for a couple of days - maybe even a week – and adopt another family for a while. An identification tag or capsule attached to the collar is useful to establish whose cat it is.

KEEP-FIT FOR CATS

Unless a cat is forced to be completely housebound by a high-rise apartment, it will take plenty of exercise naturally, in hunting, exploring and playing. All cats are kittens at heart, and at any age will enjoy jumping in and out of a cardboard box, chasing fir cones around the garden, or balls of fluff along a draughty hallway. Outdoors, they will happily climb trees, jump, stretch, pounce and roll, keeping that lithe body fit and supple. Hunting may be for real; inching along the spindliest branch of a tree or crouching for hours in a bush by the bird table to take a swipe at an unwary sparrow – sometimes fondly presenting its owner with the remains of a mouse or shrew after a night's hunting. The hunting instinct also comes out in play, especially when two cats are playing together. They will pretend to stalk and pounce, taking it in turns to roll the other over and bite the neck. You can tell that this is not serious by the way that they seem to take turns at being the attacker, and the fact that the biting never uses the teeth to pierce the skin. Two cats will always amuse each other more easily than a lone pet.

Exercising the housebound cat can take a little more planning and effort, but any cat should still be encouraged to take the initiative itself. Taught to play with cat toys such as balls, bells and cotton reels from

an early age, they should be able to amuse themselves happily enough indoors. A bored cat becomes a destructive cat and a trouble to its owner. If the cat has no access to the outdoors at all – perhaps where heavy traffic is a very real danger – it is a good idea to provide some form of climbing frame within the house or apartment. A scratching post to keep claws in trim without destroying the furniture is also recommended. For cats left alone in the house, provide them with adequate fresh air and ventilation via a special safety window catch or a wired frame that fits over the window while it is open.

Above: A couple of cats together will enjoy mock fights and boisterous games, acting quite fiercely without hurting each other in the slightest. Any form of play is an excellent form of exercise, helping to develop their natural instincts as well as keeping their bodies supple.

Left: Expensive pet toys are not essential for your cats. You will find kittens and young adult cats alike will take great delight in playing with all kinds of household rubbish, such as a screwed up ball of paper, a length of string or an old cardboard box, as here.

Right: Some cat owners without gardens will even take their cat for a walk on a lead like a dog. Not all cats will agree to being restrained in this way, and it is best to get them used to wearing a collar and being led on a lead from an early age.

Right: If your cat has access to a garden, or better still, to the wider outdoors, it will get plenty of varied exercise, such as leaping, climbing and jumping all kinds of natural obstacles. A shrubbery, woodland or even an area of long grass is a perfect playground for hunting games.

Below: A housebound cat may become bored and get into mischief if it does not get enough exercise. You should always keep an eye open for potential hazards in the home, such as an open fire or electrical flex, a temptation that most cats seem unable to resist biting.

Right: An indoor cat needs something on which to exercise its claws and scratching posts are available – like this one, which includes a play element.

Right: Fit, healthy cats have excellent muscle control and powerful back legs, which allow them to sprint and leap with great efficiency. After calculating the height of a jump by eye, the cat will crouch slightly then spring up with a thrust of its hindquarters, aiming a little beyond where it wants to land to allow the rear of the body to be drawn up on landing.

A HEALTHY CAT

Keeping your cat healthy does not necessarily mean rushing it to the veterinarian every time it looks under the weather. As a caring owner, you will soon start to recognize what upsets your pet – some have allergies and cannot digest cow's milk, for example. The healthy cat should have a sleek, glossy coat, clear bright eyes, clean dry nose and good appetite. It should move gracefully, take plenty of exercise and keep itself well groomed. If it is sick, the ears will droop, the coat become dull and matted, and the cat may go off its food. The eyes lose all sparkle and interest, and the cat may try to hide itself away. Any change in habits is an indication that something is wrong – it may be as simple as the cat drinking more or less water than usual.

Good routine maintenance is the best way to keep your cat in the peak of condition: a well-balanced diet with plenty of minerals and vitamins; daily fresh air and exercise – this is particularly important for housebound cats; and regular grooming, especially for longhaired breeds. Grooming is important, not just to keep the coat looking good, but also to check for parasites and any signs of skin disease. Routine inoculations are essential to protect your cat from the more virulent killer diseases, and a printed card or chart will not only help keep track of these, but also act as a reminder when it is time for another injection or deworming treatment.

However careful you are, active cats may still pick up disease or infection from airborne viruses, contaminated food, disease-carrying prey or faeces, even insect bites. At any sign of sneezing, vomiting, diarrhoea or discharge from the eyes or nose, you should contact a veterinarian as soon as possible, before the condition worsens.

Below: To prevent your cat scratching a head wound and thus preventing it from healing, your veterinarian may supply a special collar.

Right: Some cats are prone to getting foreign objects stuck in their mouths, particularly small bones. Removing them can be tricky and it may be necessary to seek professional help to prevent the object snapping or passing down the throat.

Left: Fresh air and exercise are essential to health, and the sight of a young active cat enjoying stalking a mouse or playing in the grass is both a pleasure and amusing for its owner.

Right: One of the signs to look out for when you suspect that your cat may be feeling under the weather is that it will eat less and drink considerably more than it normally does.

Below: Some form of carrying box is necessary to take your cat to the veterinarian. There are many different types, including this plastic case with clear sides so that your cat can see out.

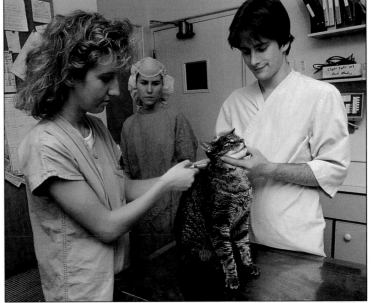

Above: When administering an injection, it is essential that the cat is restrained. If the cat struggles, the syringe may slip and hurt the cat or get damaged in the process. This is one of the reasons why most veterinarians employ at least one assistant when undertaking any kind of surgical work on your animal.

Right: Young children may be distressed at the idea of their pet being taken away to a strange place when injured or unwell, so take the time to explain carefully what is happening. Involve your child in getting the animal into its carrier and taking it to the veterinarian for treatment.

Above: The eyes sometimes become clogged with mucus and need wiping gently with a swab of clean, preferably warm, water.

Above: There are various mites and infections liable to attack your cat's ears, and they will require prompt treatment.

BREEDING YOUR CAT

You can breed pedigree cats for interest – or income, since kittens with the right characteristics will fetch a good price. Cats are relatively self reliant, so breeding is not difficult, even for a beginner, providing you decide to breed from a queen (female) and not from a stud of toms, which needs considerably more skill and experience. However, for any novice the event is worth planning carefully, especially if the female is a pedigree and you wish to register the kittens.

First, you will need to find a pedigree father with complementary characteristics, to stand a chance of producing the best possible offspring. You can find stud males through your local veterinarian or specific breed club. A fee is usually charged, dependent on results. You will know when your queen is ready to mate because she will start howling and calling. This is the time to call your chosen stud and arrange safe delivery. If mating is successful, the nipples should start reddening after about three weeks, her behaviour will become more maternal and you will notice that she will start to put on weight.

The kittens should be born about nine weeks after conception. Most queens have little problem giving· birth and do not require assistance. The exception is when labour begins prematurely (earlier than eight weeks) or later than estimated (after ten weeks). About a third of all kittens are born tail first, and this is not a cause for concern. The first indications of labour are a rapid rate of breathing and a rhythmic purring. You should try to make sure that the mother does not sneak off to a hidden spot of her own choosing to give birth, but place her gently and firmly in the kittening box, which should be prepared well in advance.

As soon as each kitten is born – they can be five minutes or several hours apart – the mother will bite off the umbilical cord. When they are all born, she will allow them to suckle. The mother should tend to all their needs for the first three weeks, after which she will encourage them to be more independent until they are fully weaned. Pedigree kittens need to be registered by the time they are a few weeks old.

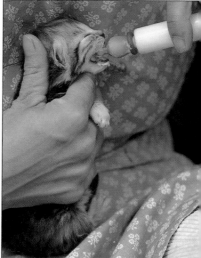

Left: Once cleaned, ensure newborn kittens are breathing and place close to the belly.

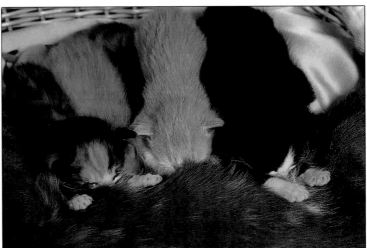

Above: If you want a particular coat and eye colour, you must choose your stud carefully. Otherwise, expect a variety of colours and markings in a litter.

Above left: Kittens start to suckle as soon as they are born. If the litter is large, you can wean the kittens on a mixture of unsweetened evaporated milk and water as soon as they can stand.

Right: At ten weeks old, a kitten is alert and mobile, with a full set of milk teeth. The coat pattern is already well defined. Eye colour changes at around 12 weeks.

Left: Handle very young kittens carefully and do not take them from the mother for long at first or she will become anxious.

Left: If the mother is unable to feed her kittens, you will need to do it yourself using a dropper, syringe or special feeding bottle. Scrupulous hygiene is essential.

Right: A pregnant cat will often find her own spot for giving birth and will shun your specially prepared kittening box for a comfortable cupboard or corner.

WHICH TYPE OF CAT?

On first acquaintance, every cat is instantly recognizable as classically cat-shaped; the cartoonist's concept of triangular head with pricked up ears and slanted eyes, sleek athletic body and sinuous tail. In fact, body shapes and types vary quite considerably, especially among purebred cats.

There are three basic variations of body shape: cobby, foreign and 'in between' variations. Cobby, flat-faced cats have a solid, almost stumpy build with short, thick legs, broad shoulders, short tail and a rounded head. Persian breeds are instantly recognizable as cobbies. Completely different in shape are the foreign type of cats: the lightly built Orientals with their long, slim legs, narrow shoulders and narrow, wedge-shaped head – all familiar traits of the Siamese. Some cats seem to fall somewhere in between, like the Maine Coon, with its more muscular body, medium-length legs and longer but slightly rounded head. Other cats are real oddities – like the tail-less Manx and the Scottish Fold, with its curious pinned down ears – but these have been developed from inbred deformities.

Length and type of fur also vary considerably, producing the different shorthair and longhair breeds, even curly-haired cats like the Rex breeds. Shorthair cats are closely related to the original wild cat, from which all cats are descended. The showy longhaired breeds, whose coats may be up to three times as long, are the result of specially refined breeding over the centuries. Within these two main types, there are other variations; for example, the long silky coat of the Angora, not quite as full as that of the fully fluffed Persian and subsequently easier to groom; the shaggy-coated Maine Coon; or the wirehaired breeds with their short curly coats.

Left: Shorthaired breeds are easier to care for, as they require less grooming and do not shed long hairs around the house. An additional advantage is that they show up colour patterns or markings to good effect. This Red Colourpoint, with contrasting mask, tail and paws, is a good example.

Right: Black is probably the most common shade among self-coloured cats. To win prizes at cat shows, the colour should be dense and glossy, with no white hairs whatsoever, no reddish brown tinge to the coat nor a smoky grey undercoat. Cross-bred with grey, black becomes blue; crossing with a brown shade gives a soft lilac.

Above: Some non-pedigree cats are particularly suited to a certain environment, simply as a result of how and where they were raised. This farm cat is perfectly at home outdoors and probably a fine hunter of small mammals, such as mice.

Left: Unless you are interested in a particular pedigree breed, colour and markings will probably be the primary factors to influence your choice of cat.

Below: Oriental shorthaired cats tend to have long sleek bodies and large pointed ears, while those with longhair blood, as here, are stockier, with a rounder, squashier face and smaller ears.

Above: The Cornish Rex is unusual in that it has a close-cropped curly coat, which makes any colour distinctive. It has long slender legs and a long tail.

Right: The distinctive feature of a Calico cat is its strongly defined tortoiseshell-and-white markings, which make it look like patchwork. The pattern shows up best on a shorthaired breed.

SELECTING BY DESIGN

Cats come in an extraordinary range of colours across the different breeds, from blues and lilacs to golds and chocolates, with wonderful striped, spotted and banded markings. Some are highly prized and demand high prices. Others are sought simply through personal preference, or perhaps because they match a decorating scheme in the house! New colours and combinations are still being introduced by enterprising breeders every year.

When the cat is a single colour – such as black, white or brown, with no pattern, shading or ticking – it is classed as self- or solid-coloured. Best known is the all-black cat, which occurs in all types of both longhair and shorthair breeds. Equally popular is the completely white cat, sometimes a true albino with pink eyes, but more often with blue or deep orange eyes. Cats may also be totally blue, chestnut brown, cinnamon brown, lilac, cream or red. The popular tabby markings form a variety of striped and spotted patterns. The cat might be mackerel striped like a tiger, or spotted, blotched or ticked in any one of a wide range of stunning colour combinations. The black on silver spotted tabby is particularly handsome, although the brown and red varieties are more familiar. These colour variations are inherited from the cat's wild ancestors, and are a most efficient form of camouflage, even in the suburban backyard.

For the breeder and cat show enthusiast, there are fancier cat colour effects, especially among the longhair breeds. Coats may be subtly shaded or tipped in a secondary colour, which looks particularly fine in the smoky grey and silver colours but is also pretty in red and cream markings. Siamese are famous for their coloured 'points' – darker markings on nose, ears, feet and tail. Here, again, there is a wide choice of different colours, including tabby and tortoiseshell patterns, at the points. Most complex are the multicoloured cats, such as the piebald black-and-white, the black-and-orange tortoiseshell, and the 'patched tabby' – sometimes called a tabby tortie or torbie – with its complicated multicoloured markings.

Below: The tortoiseshell-and-white markings of the Calico cat are usually strongly contrasted. Particularly popular in the USA.

Right: The Russian Blue is a beautiful silver blue colour enhanced by its plush coat. Blue is a very popular cat colour.

Right: Tabby markings take one of two pattern forms: the Classic, or blotched effect, and Mackerel, which is more tiger-striped. Brown- and red-based colours are the best known, but there is a wide range of shades based on the self-colours, including blue, chocolate, lilac and cream.

Left: Black-and-white is one of the most popular colour combinations in domestic cats. It appears in a range of markings: bibs and socks, blazes, stripes and splashes on the head.

Below: All-white cats are popular pets and come in only three varieties: blue- copper- or odd-eyed. A rich orange or brilliant sapphire blue eye colour is preferred for showing.

Above: Pure white cats often have odd-coloured eyes: one blue and one yellow, which looks unusual but is not rare. The blue-eyed all-white cat is prone to deafness in most breeds.

Left: Red and cream coloration occurs in both longhaired and shorthaired cats. Paler shades are preferred for showing, but it is rare to achieve a uniform self-colour in this group, as some tabby markings are usually seen on face, legs and tail. In long-haired breeds, the thick coat helps even out the basic shade.

British and American Shorthairs

Right: The Exotic Shorthair is a new good-natured breed, with the stocky body and flattened face of a Persian and a short, manageable coat in a wide choice of around 40 colours and patterns. A loving, lively cat.

With their wonderful variety of colours and patterns, shorthaired cats offer plenty of choice to cat lovers with busy lifestyles, looking for an intelligent, good-natured companion that requires minimum care and grooming. Their short, dense coats display strong colour variations, such as tabby and spotted markings, very well. The fur does not tangle or mat, and simply needs a quick brush through twice a week to keep it in prime condition.

British Shorthairs tend to have a sturdy muscular body with a broad, rounded head and large, round eyes. The American Shorthair, believed to be introduced to the Americas by the first Pilgrim Fathers and, as a result, a good, hardy cat, is slightly different to look at: larger and longer with a more oval head and squarer muzzle. Some of the most beautiful British Shorthairs feature spectacular markings and include tabbies, tortoiseshells and the striking 'Spottie', with its black-spotted silver or brown coat. There is also a red-spotted version. Equally popular is the Bicolour, with its patches of white – often in the form of bib and mittens – on a black, blue, red or cream coat. The powerful American Shorthair offers a similarly large choice of shades and patterns – from the golden-eyed Blue Smoke, its white fur tipped with deep blue, to single colours, tortoiseshells and tabbies.

Almost in a class of its own but closely related to the American Shorthairs is the pretty American Wirehair, distinguished by its curled woolly coat but featuring the same athletic body and good colour variations. There is a new breed that combines the plush coat of an American Shorthair with the stockier body and wide flat face of one of the longhaired breeds. Called the Exotic Shorthair, it is the perfect compromise if you like the shape and expression of a Persian but wish to avoid the moulting hairs and daily grooming that Persians involve.

Below: The American Red Tabby Shorthair has golden eyes and a rich red-coloured coat, with the Classic tabby or Mackerel markings in a much darker red. Overall, an attractive and athletic-looking cat.

Left: Selective breeding of Shorthairs has resulted in a wide choice of varieties. Blue with its copper or orange-coloured eyes is very popular. The sturdy body is stocky and muscular. The American Shorthair tends to have longer legs and a larger, leaner body.

Right: The American Wire-hair is the result of a natural mutation that occurred in a litter of American Shorthairs in the 1970s. They have a curious crimped woolly coat.

Below: The pure White Shorthair is gentle and affectionate. It has a stocky muscular body and large blue or gold eyes. As in Longhairs, Blue-eyed White Shorthairs are prone to deafness. Odd-eyed individuals are also found.

FOREIGN SHORTHAIRS

Some owners prefer their cats to have that sleek and elegant 'foreign' build typified by the Siamese: a slim, athletic body, with long legs and dainty feet, wedge-shaped head with large pointed ears and lovely almond-shaped eyes. To meet this demand, the Siamese has been crossed with domestic shorthair varieties to produce a fine-looking cat with a soft coat, sporting none of the familiar Siamese point markings but available in twelve plain, smoke and patterned coat types. Distinctive, with its chestnut-coloured short coat and Siamese-type build, is the Havana Brown. And there is the Tonkinese, a pretty Siamese/Burmese cross that faintly retains the point markings and is bred in five subtle mink shades. Even more striking is the Snowshoe, with its much darker mask, ears and legs, and dainty white feet. A cross between a Siamese and a bicolour American Shorthair, the Snowshoe comes in two varieties: the fawn Seal-point and the grey-blue Blue-point. All these breeds have happily inherited the lively and affectionate nature of the Siamese, as well as its oriental elegance, and, like the Siamese, need plenty of attention.

If you are looking for a good-looking cat with a loving disposition, the Bombay is for you: a black American Shorthair crossed with Burmese, its short fur is a wonderful, glossy jet black and its round eyes a rich gold. This cat is happiest in company and is therefore the ideal companion for an elderly person. The same applies to the Singapura – a quiet, friendly cat with large slanted eyes and a slight but stocky body. An oriental import, the Singapura is distinguished by its fabulous short silky fur in pale beige, with bands of dark bronze and cream ticking.

Left: The tabby patterned Oriental Shorthair is a relatively recent introduction, developed to meet the need for a tabby with a Siamese body shape. Oriental Tabbies were granted breed recognition in 1978 to distinguish them from the American-bred Egyptian Mau.

Right: The Havana is a bright, lively cat that enjoys plenty of attention. A rich chocolate brown colour with almond-shaped green eyes, it is named not after the cigars, but after a breed of rabbits of the same shade. This self-coloured breed was first developed in the 1950s.

Left: The pretty Singapura looks rather like an Abyssinian but is much smaller, probably due to its origins as a scavenging street cat. It is also wary of humans. In Singapore, cats are unpopular and this one lives in the city's drains, hence its common name of 'drain cat'.

Left: The Tonkinese, a popular show cat, is a mink-coloured cross between a Siamese and a Burmese. There are two other colours: a honey mink shade and a blue-grey. All the cats have blue-green eyes.

Above: Some solid colours occur naturally in Siamese litters, but matings between two known varieties of self-coloured brown cats can produce the Black or Ebony Shorthair. Its short, fine coat should be totally jet black and the eyes slanted and bright green. The Black, acknowledged in 1978, is one of only 12 recognized varieties of Oriental Shorthair, although many have been developed.

Left: The rare silver-blue Korat has a short silky coat, huge round green eyes and a pretty heart-shaped face. Kittens have yellow or amber eyes.

Below: The all-White Oriental with blue eyes was developed in the 1960s. It does not have the tendency to deafness of other blue-eyed white cats.

SIAMESE CATS

In addition to its highly distinctive looks, the Siamese has a most extraordinary personality that has endeared it to cat lovers for centuries. It was certainly a favourite at the Royal Court of Siam as long ago as the sixth century, but was probably not finally established in Europe until the nineteenth century. It first appeared in North American shows earlier this century.

Many consider the Siamese to be the height of grace and beauty in the cat world, with its long slim legs, small paws and wedge-shaped head with long, aristocratic nose. The ears are long and pointed, seemingly always pricked to attention, and the beautiful almond-shaped eyes are a stunning blue. The coat is short, fine and soft, with the familiar dark markings called 'points' on the ears, mask, tail and paws. The four classic colours are: Seal-point (cream and brown), Blue-point (pale and slate blue), Chocolate-point (brown on ivory) and the stylish Lilac-point, with grey-pink markings on a creamy, pink-tinged coat. New colours have been introduced by mating Siamese with other breeds, and these are called Colourpoint Shorthairs to distinguish them. These include interesting tabby and tortoiseshell varieties.

Unmistakable to look at, the Siamese's behaviour is equally unique among cats. Its extrovert nature makes the cat a fairly demanding pet, but an expressively affectionate one. It needs a home where it will receive plenty of attention. This is one of few cats that can be trained almost like a dog to walk on a leash, turn somersaults and retrieve. If discontented or jealous of a rival, Siamese cats let the whole neighbourhood know with the most heart-rending yowling.

Above: The Red-point Siamese is a lovely new variety, with a white to apricot-shaded coat and reddish gold markings. It was originally bred by mating Siamese with other breeds.

Left: Siamese cats have a cheeky and extrovert nature that makes them lovable if rather demanding pets, as well as popular show animals. They enjoy exercise and fresh air.

Right: This Tabby- or Lynx-point is one of several new colours recognized in Siamese cats. The early kittens bred were seal-coloured, but now a full range of shades is possible.

Above: Lilac-point, or Frost-point, Siamese cats result from combining blue and chocolate brown genes. The magnolia coat has pinkish grey markings.

Right: Whatever its coat colour, the Siamese is distinguished by its slanted, almond-shaped, bright blue eyes and long nose in a wedge-shaped head.

Right: The first Blue-point Siamese was registered as long ago as last century, but did not receive official recognition until the 1930s. Breeding between the Blue self-coloured Siamese and a Seal-point has produced an attractive cat with a bluish white coat and darker slate-blue tail, paws and mask.

Below: The Chocolate-point Siamese, with its soft ivory coat and brown markings, was one of the first varieties to be bred.

47

BURMESE CATS

Long-lived and loving, the playful Burmese makes an excellent and handsome shorthaired companion in town or country. It is a breed with a well-documented history, beginning in 1930 when a walnut brown female called Wong Mau was brought back to the United States from Rangoon. In the absence of any male Burmese, she was mated with the nearest breed type – which happened to be Siamese; then the resulting kittens were cross-bred to get back as close as possible to the original all-over chocolate colour. Today, the breed is well established and nine colours have been introduced, including Blue, Lilac, Red, Cream and Tortoiseshell varieties, all of which retain the strikingly slanted golden eyes.

In some countries, there is a certain reluctance to accept these new shades, and only the traditional brown is considered to be a true Burmese. Specifications as to ideal body shape and size also vary, but generally, the Burmese has a fairly large, muscular type of body with long slim legs and dainty paws. Like the body, the ears are shorter and more rounded than those of a Siamese, and while they have high cheekbones, the nose is much shorter. American breeders prefer the head, body and eyes to be rounder than their British counterparts.

Burmese tend to be less noisy and nervous than the highly refined Siamese, yet they share the same athletic nature and love of fun that makes them amusing and entertaining pets. There are longhaired versions of the Burmese called Tiffanies, which combine the rich chocolate colouring of the original with a long, silky coat and spectacular neck ruff.

Above: Although the Brown – sometimes called the British Brown – Burmese is considered by some to be the only true Burmese, other colours are recognized and the Blue is particularly popular. Its coat is a beautiful silver-grey with sheeny markings. The eyes are yellow.

Left: Reds, Creams and Tortoiseshells are relatively new colours among the Burmese. They were created in the 1970s by cross-breeding with a Red-point Siamese, a shorthaired ginger tabby, and a tortoiseshell-and-white farm cat. Today, self-coloured coats and a selection of tortie variations are possible.

Left: The Cream Burmese is one of the attractive new colours. It is a rich but much paler shade than in other cat breeds, with no markings at all on the coat. Blue Tortoiseshell Burmese are a mixture of Blue and Cream and, again, the colours look much paler than in other breeds.

Right: This pale Lilac Burmese was first bred in the USA, where it is called Platinum. It is a pale dove grey with a pink tinge, but the kittens are almost white when born and do not colour until several weeks old. Forelegs are shorter than hind legs; paws small and oval.

Below: According to cat breed organizations, Brown – or Sable, as the colour is called in North America – is the main Burmese variety. To achieve show standard, the coat should be short, thick and glossy, the body rounded and muscular with long slim legs and the ears widely set, with rounded points.

Left: In North America, the Chocolate is more frequently called Champagne and is a pale milk chocolate with a darker shaded head. Some breeders do not like the contrast of colours.

EXOTIC CATS

Some cats are so striking in their appearance, with a particularly expressive face, beautiful fine fur or graceful elegance, that they immediately stand out as a breed apart. A few of these exotic breeds are rare; other groups are so popular that they demand their own nationwide cat shows. The lovely Abyssinian and its longhaired cousin, the Somali, belong to this second group. It is easy to see why they demand so much attention. The Abyssinian is related to the superbly elegant cats once worshipped by the Ancient Egyptians. It has a lithe and slender physique, with a rounded, wedge-shaped head and wonderfully intelligent expression. The thick, short fur can be one of three charming pattern types: copper-red ticked with chocolate brown, blue-grey ticked with steely blue, and light brown marked in a darker shade.

The smart Russian Blue also has an attractive thick, short fur with a real sheen to it. However, as its name implies, the colour of the coat is a fabulous silver blue. This quiet, obliging cat actually prefers to be confined indoors. Another cat with an affectionate character and outstanding coat – so fine that it often attracts cat thieves – is the Egyptian Mau. Four varieties feature the magnificent dark-spotted markings: grey on silver,

brown on honey, black on grey and grey on fawn. Similar in build to the Abyssinian, the Egyptian Mau is also believed to have been specially bred in imitation of the cat worshipped by the Egyptians. The exotic Ocicat, bred from a Siamese/Abyssinian cross, shows a similar coat pattern – hence its name, after the wild ocelot. A large, muscular cat, the Ocicat is usually a rich blend of browns and bronzes. Silky, silver blue and very rare, the Korat is another unusual cat, with its beautiful heart-shaped face, large green eyes and peaceful, loving nature.

Left: The Somali has the same attractively ticked coat as the Abyssinian, but much longer, silky hair. Some have much longer coats than others. The tail is usually bushy and full, yet the coat is generally easy to groom.

Above: A pair of Korats was once considered a good luck symbol for Thai brides, and this lovely but rare silver-blue cat, with its large, bright green eyes, is certainly a striking gift. It has a quiet and affectionate nature.

Left: The elegant Abyssinian is a medium-sized cat with a short, extremely thick coat, usually coloured a pale ruddy brown or black. There is also a Sorrel (Red) and a Blue variety.

Right: The combination of a double coat and a blue colour tipped with silver, produces a luxurious sheen in the fur of this Russian Blue. Quiet and contented, this breed is ideally suited to an indoor life.

Below: Prized for its distinctive, beautiful, sleek spotted coat, the Egyptian Mau has a muscular body and alert expression.

Below: The Bronze Egyptian Mau reveals a more subtle but extremely sophisticated pattern of dark brown spots – in fact, a series of broken stripes – on a honey shaded background. The almond-shaped eyes are green.

Left: In this young cat, a Mau's distinctive spotted markings can be more clearly seen as broken stripes and bands. Later, it will develop the stunning contrasted coat and elegant body shape of the adult. This silver colouring with black markings is particularly pretty.

PERSIANS – PLAIN AND SIMPLE

Persian cats are instantly familiar and much loved, with their large, round eyes in a broadly whiskered face, and stocky body covered in long, soft silky fur. They are the classic longhaired cats, probably first known in Europe as long as three hundred years ago, and certainly a regular entrant in cat shows for over a century. They were introduced to North America around the end of the nineteenth century, where they quickly became popular. It is not just their beautiful coat and funny, almost cross-eyed expression that makes them so appealing. Persians are bred in a spectacular rainbow of colours and markings, which can make choosing one a really difficult task.

The earliest breeds were the self-, or solid, colours: totally black, white, cream, blue or orange. The Whites were the first longhaired cats to be introduced to Europe, and are prized for their blue eyes, although Orange-eyed Whites sometimes occur. There is also a rarer odd-eyed version – with one eye of each colour. The White remains popular, and no doubt the much rarer Black would be more popular if it did not tend to develop a brownish tinge and require a great deal of grooming. The Red Persian is really stunning: a deep rich colour, with small tufty ears, although it is rarely pure and clear of markings. Other Persian self-colours include cream, various shades of blue, and a very pretty (and usually female) pastel blue and cream cross-breed. More recent colours include a delicious dark chocolate and a soft lilac.

There is a curious variety in the red and red tabby Persian colours with a comical squashed face, which is appropriately called the Peke-faced Persian or Longhair. These are like any other Persian breed in shape and coat, but feature a very short nose and an indentation between the eyes, which produces the striking similarity to a Pekinese dog and, incidentally, makes them prone to breathing difficulties.

Right: The Smoke-coloured Persian looks a solid colour, but in fact has a pale undercoat with dark tips, which produces a shimmering effect. There are two varieties, a black- and a blue-tipped; both have orange eyes.

Above: Cream is one of the earliest solid colours and has large copper-coloured eyes.

Right: The Red Persian is the rarest solid colour. Ideally, there should be no tabby markings.

Left: The Blue Self-coloured kitten may show faint tabby markings when born, but these fade after a few months. Various shades of blue are produced, although the paler varieties are preferred for showing.

Right: A true Black is quite rare, as damp weather and strong sunshine can produce a brown tinge. Kittens are often naturally speckled and may not develop a jet black coat for six months.

Above: The all-White Persian, was the first longhaired cat to be introduced to Europe. Odd-eyed Whites have one blue and one orange eye. The blue-eyed is prone to deafness.

Right: Blue is the most popular Persian Self-colour. The colour can range from dark to light and the eyes are always copper-coloured. Its body shape is nearest to the ideal show standard of any Persian.

PERSIANS – PATTERNED, SHADED AND TIPPED

The Persian's thick coat and stocky body shape show off many multicolour variations to full effect. This is particularly true of the Tortoiseshell, sometimes called a 'Tortie' Persian. The dense silky coat is a fabulous blend of deep red, black and cream; the eyes are a brilliant orange or copper colour. Even more striking, perhaps, is the Tortoiseshell-and-White, which has bold white patches to highlight the red, cream and black. It looks so like a piece of printed cotton patchwork that it is often called a Calico cat. For anyone looking for a big fluffy cat to blend with a modern decorative scheme, there is a variation – the Dilute Calico – in which the patchy colour is translated into pretty pastel tones of blue, cream and white. Persians may have both striped and blotched tabby patterns and, although the reds and browns are attractive, it is the silver tabby that is most prized for its stunning silver-grey markings.

There are a great many other coloured categories, depending on the strength and distribution of the colour. Some are as subtle as the Smoke Persian, where every hair in a mainly white coat is tipped with a dark grey or blue secondary colour, creating a shimmering effect as the cat moves. A pure white coat tipped with black is called Chinchilla after the South American rodent, and tipping with red, cream, tabby or tortoiseshell produces the Cameo pattern. This can be short tipped, producing a soft fuzz of colour called Shell Cameo, or have longer colour tips to produce the beautiful Shaded Cameo.

The Bicolours are a cross between white and another single colour, ideally producing the effect of a sparkling white shirt front, and are bred in any of the recognized shades. In the pedigree world it can be difficult to achieve the symmetrical pattern that the show standard demands. There is a Bicolour variation in which the head and tail alone are coloured, and these have been named Persian Vans after their similarity to Turkish Van markings.

Left: The Tortoiseshell-and-white is an attractive Persian with the traditional Tortie colouring, plus white patches and copper or orange eyes. Its distinctive appearance, similar to printed cotton, has given it the name Calico cat in the USA. A female only variety.

Right: There are five recognized varieties of Tabby Persian: Red, Brown, Silver, Blue and Cream, displaying either the Classic or Mackerel pattern. They are difficult to breed successfully; in the long thick fur, the pattern does not show up as well as it would in a shorthaired breed.

Below: Black and Blue solid-coloured Persians are crossed with a Chinchilla to produce the silky thick-coated Smoke, which has long dark fur and a pale dark-tipped undercoat. Varieties include a Black and Blue.

Right: Difficult to breed and, therefore, expensive to buy, the Tortoiseshell, or Tortie, Persian is a rich mixture of red, cream and black patches with large round copper or orange eyes. Always female, they are particularly prized if they have a cream or red blaze running from nose to forehead. The variety is believed to be an accidental cross between Persians and tortie shorthairs.

Left: The Dilute Calico sports a similar patchwork effect to its fluffy coat as the Tortie-and-white, but in softer, more subtle shades. It is sometimes classed as the Blue-cream-and-white Persian. An appealing cat.

Above: The Chinchilla has a beautiful white silky coat tipped with black, and huge emerald or blue-green eyes. There is a variety called the Shaded Silver, which is slightly darker in colour and has green eyes.

NEW LONGHAIRS

For those who love the sleek elegance of lithe oriental cats, but fancy a pet with a splendid long coat, some of the new longhair breeds manage to combine the best of both worlds. Several are simply longhair versions of popular shorter-haired cats such as the Balinese – a longhair Siamese with the same agile habits, wedge-shaped head and bright blue eyes. Others have originated from areas with a particularly cold climate so that they have naturally developed long coats.

These new breeds tend to be rather slimmer and more elegant in body and face than the chunky Persian longhairs. And because their single coat is not quite as woolly, they are much easier to groom. The Birman, for example, has long silky fur and the most beautiful colouring: a pale gold, short-legged body with dark mask, ears, tail and legs, plus distinctive white gloves on its paws. The equally attractive Somali is really a longhaired Abyssinian with the same rich red golden colouring ticked with bands of dark hairs. Its coat is thick and silky but easy to groom, and the tail is bushy. Another bushy-tailed cat with fine long fur is the re-introduced Angora, or Turkish Angora, related to a very ancient breed of cat. It has a long slim body, attractive wedge-shaped head and a variety of colours from black and grey to blue, red, brown and silver tabby variations. Similar in style but stockier in build is the auburn Turkish cat, sometimes called a Turkish Van, which has a most unusual red-and-white coloured coat. Completely different but hugely popular for its thick, shaggy, rather rough coat and wide range of colour markings, is the Maine Coon. Originally developed from a hardy American farm cat crossed with Angoras, this large but friendly cat makes a super pet, although it needs plenty of space and access to a garden or backyard.

Above: Developed in response to the demand for a Siamese-patterned cat with the long silky hair and stocky body of a Persian, the Himalayan is available in many colours: Seal-point, Blue-point, Chocolate-point, Lilac-point, Red-point, and all shades of Tortie- and Tabby-point.

Right: The Colourpoint, or Himalayan is easily recognized by its soft silky coat with a pale body colour and dense point markings. The thickness of the coat prevents it from achieving the strong colour contrasts of the Siamese.

Left: The rough, shaggy Maine Coon, descended from a breed of wild cat, takes its name from its strong resemblance to the raccoon's own heavy fur coat.

Below: Although it has long silky fur, the Angora does not have the thick fluffy undercoat of standard Longhair breeds and is, therefore, far easier to groom.

Above: Beautiful brown-gold or blue-grey markings distinguish the gentle, friendly Birman. The body is long and muscular, the head broad-faced and rounded. It will mix well with other pets.

Above: Himalayan cats have small litters and their kittens are fluffy rather than longhaired until they reach maturity.

Right: The quite rare Tabby Longhairs can be Classic or, as here, Mackerel patterned. This silver variety has black markings and green or hazel eyes.

UNUSUAL CATS

Curiosities occur among all animals – strange mutations or variations of size, shape and colour that produce a real oddity, sometimes barely recognizable as the same species. Cats are no exception, and there are several breeds maintained for their appeal to those who are fascinated by the unusual or the bizarre.

Strangest, and probably rarest, is the Sphynx, a completely hairless cat with a long, slender body and tail. It looks more like a large rodent than a cat. Originally bred in Canada, the hairless skin of the Sphynx occurs in all the familiar colours and patterns, with a fine covering of down on the face, ears, paws and the end of the tail. There are also two breeds of curly-coated cats with fur so short and fine that the kittens look almost hairless. These are the Cornish and Devon Rex, which have very similar characteristics but are not, in fact, related. The Devon Rex has a pointed pixie face and slim body, which makes its large pointed ears look even bigger. Its tight curly coat and habit of wagging its tail have earned it the nickname 'poodle cat'. The Cornish Rex has a much finer, silkier fur and the classic wedge-shaped head. Even the Rex's whiskers are curly, and either breed can occur in any of the full range of colours and patterns.

Other cats have curious tails; the Manx is famous for having no tail at all. A shorthaired, intelligent cat, the Manx can be either the 'Rumpy' type, with no visible tail; or 'Stumpy', with a rudimentary stump. The Manx occurs in any shorthair colours and markings and there is also a pretty longhaired variety called the Cymric. The Japanese Bobtail is equally famous for its strange

tail mutation; the short and curly hair grows in all directions, producing an unusual fluffy effect, like a rabbit's powder puff tail. It is the ears that distinguish the Scottish Fold; they flop forward close to the head like a cap, producing an amusing round-headed effect and a surprised expression.

Above: The curious Manx not only has no tail, but its hind legs are shorter than its forelegs, making it look and move rather like a rabbit. The true Manx is the 'Rumpy' variety, which has a small hollow where the tail should be. It is believed to have proliferated in the Isle of Man from a natural mutant.

Left: The Japanese Bobtail is also distinguished by its curious tail, which is short, fluffy and curled. A wide range of coat colours is possible, but the Tortoiseshell-and-white, known as Mi-Ke, is considered lucky. This muscular cat has a friendly and intelligent expression.

Above: An extremely short curly coat with a soft silky feel gives the Cornish Rex a delicate appearance, but in fact this is a playful, energetic cat. All the recognized shorthair colour variations are possible.

Right: The rare Sphynx is gentle and friendly, but does not enjoy being handled. Its hairless coat looks like soft suede, and it has huge rounded ears and a long-tailed body.

Above: What an odd-looking cat the Scottish Fold is! The ears are folded so close to the head they look more like an owl's and its solemn expression only emphasizes its comical look. The degree to which the ears lie close to the head varies. A wide range of colours is available.

Below: The longhaired Manx, or Cymric, originated in North America and did not appear in litters until the 1960s. It was established as a separate breed in the 1970s. The attractive silky coat is thick and of medium length, appearing in a range of colours, including tabbies.

59

INDEX

Page numbers in **bold** indicate major references, including accompanying photographs. Page numbers in *italics* indicate captions to other illustrations. Less important text entries are shown in normal type.

PICTURE CREDITS